Atlanta BRAVES

KENNY ABDO

Fly!
An Imprint of Abdo Zoom
abdobooks.com

abdobooks.com

Published by Abdo Zoom, a division of ABDO, P.O. Box 398166, Minneapolis, Minnesota 55439.

Printed in the United States of America, North Mankato, Minnesota.
102025
012026

Photo Credits: Alamy, AP Images, Bridgeman Images, Getty Images, Shutterstock
Production Contributors: Kenny Abdo, Jennie Forsberg, Grace Hansen
Design Contributors: Candice Keimig, Neil Klinepier

Library of Congress Control Number: 2025936765

Publisher's Cataloging-in-Publication Data

Names: Abdo, Kenny, author.
Title: Atlanta Braves / by Kenny Abdo
Description: Minneapolis, Minnesota : Abdo Zoom, 2026 | Series: MLB teams | Includes online resources and index.
Identifiers: ISBN 9798384940104 (lib. bdg.) | ISBN 9798384940869 (ebook) | ISBN 9798384941248 (read-to-me ebook)
Subjects: LCSH: Atlanta Braves (Baseball team)--Juvenile literature. | Baseball teams--Juvenile literature. | Professional sports--Juvenile literature. | Sports franchises--Juvenile literature. | Major League Baseball (Organization)--Juvenile literature.
Classification: DDC 796.357--dc23

Table of CONTENTS

BRAVES

With a history stretching more than 150 years, a treasure trove of World Series titles, and unforgettable players, the story of the Atlanta Braves is a home run.

As a team of powerful hitters and broken **records**, the Braves bring energy and excitement to the game through fearless play.

BATTER UP!

The team began in 1871 as the Boston Red Stockings. They joined the **National League** (**NL**) in 1876 and became the Braves in 1912. Today, they are the longest-running professional team in Major League Baseball (MLB).

BOSTON

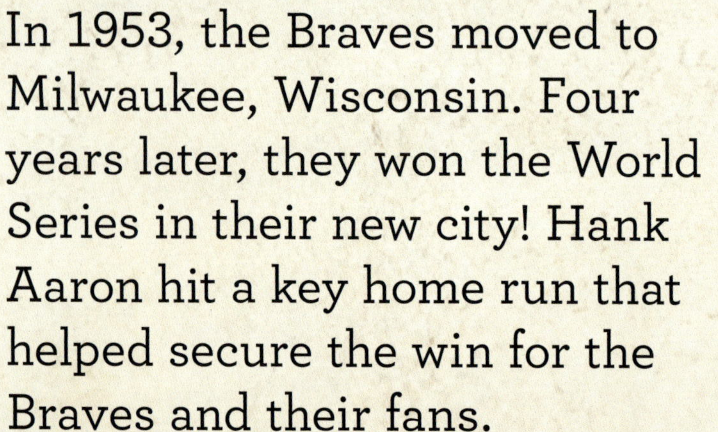

In 1953, the Braves moved to Milwaukee, Wisconsin. Four years later, they won the World Series in their new city! Hank Aaron hit a key home run that helped secure the win for the Braves and their fans.

44

The Braves moved to Atlanta, Georgia, in 1966 and gained a loyal group of fans. By the 1990s, the team became one of the best in baseball. With **manager** Bobby Cox leading the way, the Braves won their **division** 14 years in a row. No other team in MLB history has done that.

690
SPORTS
690
SPORTS

GRAND SLAMS

In 1995, the Braves won the World Series! It was their first championship win since moving to Atlanta. Pitchers Greg Maddux and Tom Glavine played major roles in the team's victory over the Guardians.

By 2005, the Braves had been one of the top teams in the **NL** East. Chipper Jones stayed strong in the lineup for years. In 2010, Freddie Freeman joined the team and became a star. From 2006 to 2019, the Braves made the playoffs six times. In 2019, they won 97 games and took first place in their **division**.

In Game 1 of the 2020 **Wild Card Series**, Freddie Freeman hit a **walk-off single** in the 13th inning to beat the Reds. The Braves kept the Reds scoreless for 22 straight innings, breaking the **record** set by the Giants in 1921.

FREEMAN
5

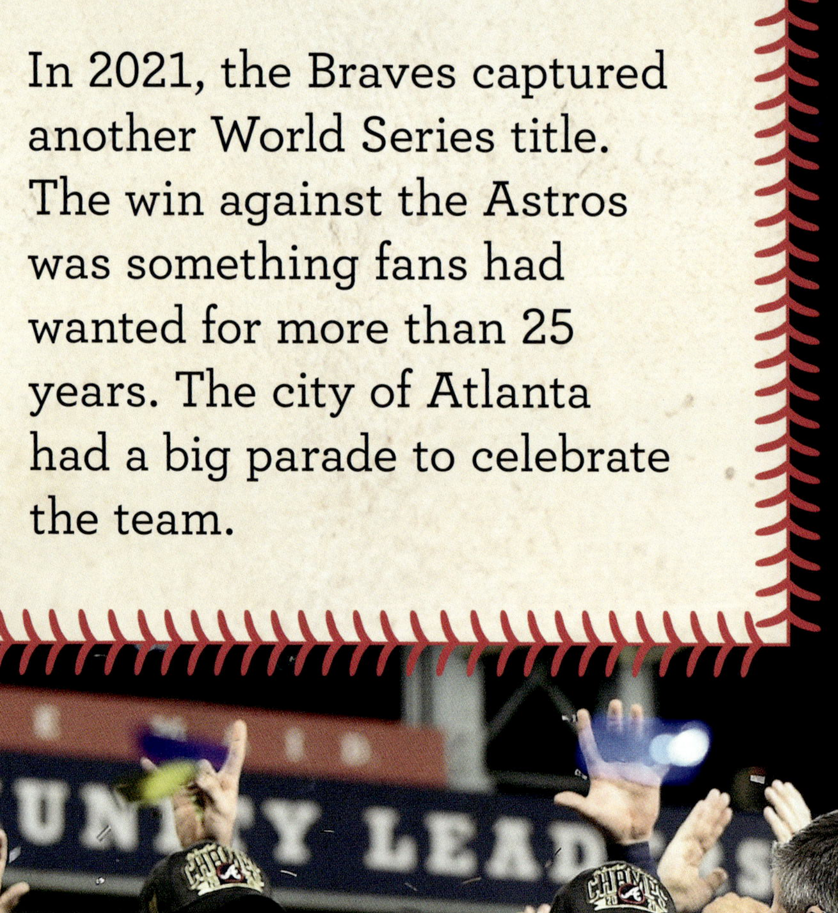

In 2021, the Braves captured another World Series title. The win against the Astros was something fans had wanted for more than 25 years. The city of Atlanta had a big parade to celebrate the team.

CHAMPIONS

In 2024, Chris Sale made Braves history by winning the **Triple Crown**. He led the league in wins, strikeouts, and **ERA**. Sale also earned a **Gold Glove**, was named Comeback Player of the Year, and made the All-MLB First Team. To top it off, he won his first **Cy Young Award**.

Braves

HALL OF FAME

Hank Aaron is a Braves legend. He broke Babe Ruth's home run **record** with 733 while with the team. Aaron's powerful hitting made him one of the greatest players in baseball history. He was named to the Baseball Hall of Fame in 1982.

Braves
44

Chipper Jones spent his entire career with the Braves. He was a powerful switch-hitter who helped the team win many games. Jones won MVP in 1999. He finished his career with 2,726 hits and eight **All-Star Game** appearances. Jones entered the Baseball Hall of Fame in 2018.

Braves
SPORTSOUTH

Atlanta

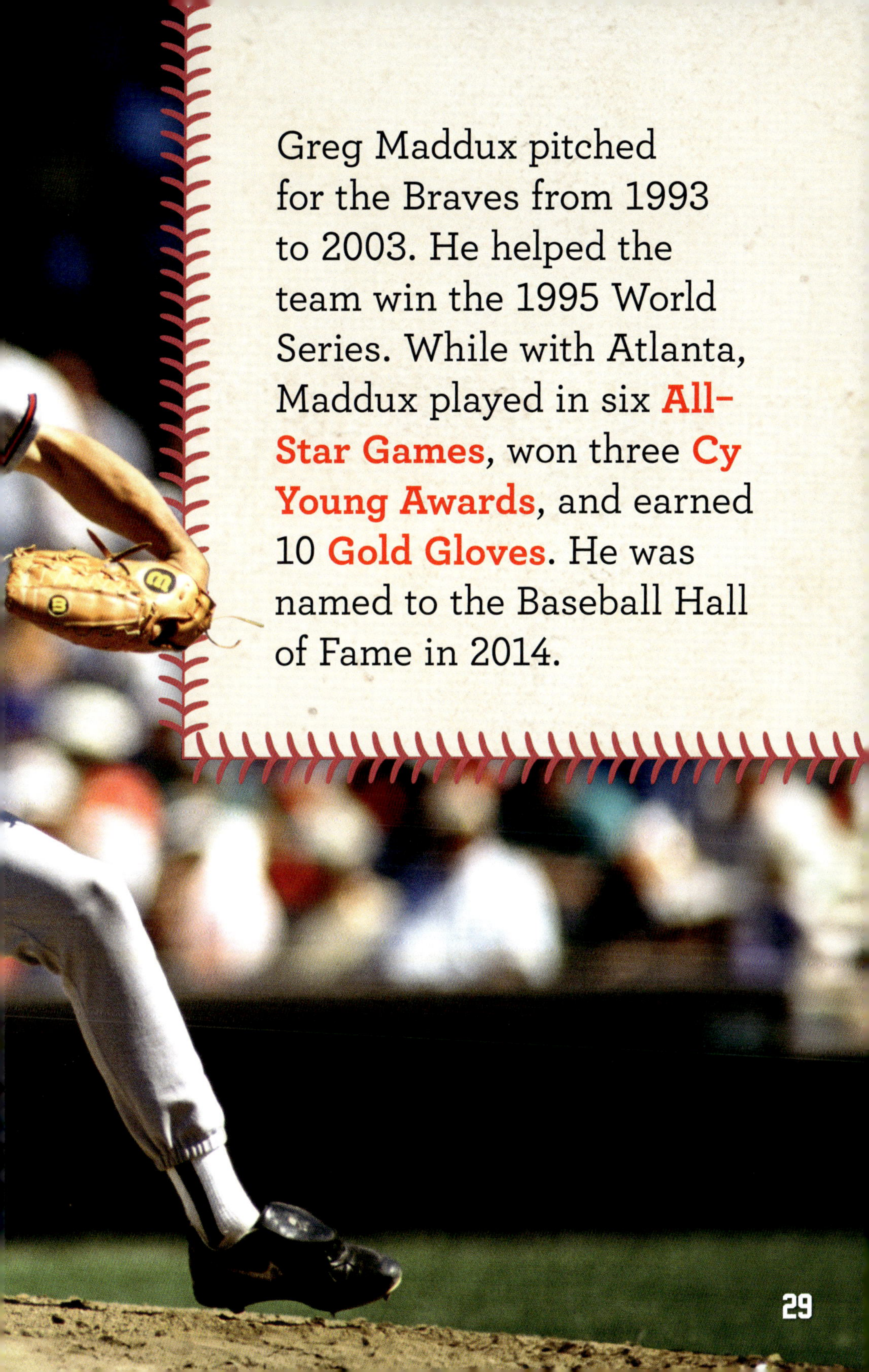

Greg Maddux pitched for the Braves from 1993 to 2003. He helped the team win the 1995 World Series. While with Atlanta, Maddux played in six **All-Star Games**, won three **Cy Young Awards**, and earned 10 **Gold Gloves**. He was named to the Baseball Hall of Fame in 2014.

GLOSSARY

All-Star Game – a yearly baseball contest where top players from the American League (AL) and the NL compete against each other.

Cy Young Award – an annual American baseball award given to the best pitcher in each of the two MLB leagues.

division – a number of teams grouped together in a sport for competitive purposes.

Earned-Run Average (ERA) – the average number of earned runs per game scored against a pitcher.

Gold Glove Award – an annual award given to the best fielders at each position in both the AL and NL.

manager – also called a field manager, a position on a baseball team that is equivalent to head coach.

National League (NL) – one of two 15-team leagues that make up MLB.

record – a top achievement by a player or team that no one has done before.

Triple Crown – an achievement earned when leading the league in batting average, home runs, and runs batted in (RBIs) in the same season.

walk-off single – a hit (where the batter safely reaches first base) that drives in the winning run in the bottom of the final inning.

Wild Card Series – the first round of the postseason.

ONLINE RESOURCES

To learn more about the Atlanta Braves, please visit **abdobooklinks.com** or scan this QR code. These links are routinely monitored and updated to provide the most current information available.

INDEX